ZOOM FOR

BEGINNERS

The Absolute Step-by-Step Beginner's Guide to Quickly Get Started with Zoom and Run Successful Classes and Virtual Meetings

TABLE OF CONTENTS

Introduction

People around the world are advancing into the digital world at an exponential rate, so much so that a major part of their day is driven by technology and digital devices. Our cell phones, watches, books, televisions, and even faucets are cutting-edge and powered by technology. Our work environment has also witnessed a massive impact through shifting to digital tools that make our lives easier.

One such technology that has made our professional and personal lives better is video conferencing. It has increased our work efficiency, saved time and money, enhanced productivity, and brought about more convenience. The modern era has made it possible to connect with almost anyone in the world through this virtual platform.

With recent social distancing practices, a lot of people have turned toward Zoom, which is a video conferencing service that allows multiple users to participate in virtual meetings. You too can use Zoom to connect to your loved ones or conduct virtual business meetings. If you are new to this platform, this book will guide you through all aspects of Zoom - what it is, its features, how to use it, and some additional tips.

While learning the practical aspects of operating a video call and service is important, there are also certain contextual aspects that one must know before leading any virtual meeting. To help you with this, the latter section of this book will teach you ways to be a pro in a video conference along with certain dos and don'ts that will make you an ace in this arena.

But, before we delve into these specifics, you should learn the merit and authority of video conferencing within all spheres.

The Increasing Importance of Technology and Video Conferencing

Before we discuss the importance of technology and video conferencing, let's first talk about what video conferencing actually is. At its most basic, video conferencing consists of virtual online meetings that are held over video conferencing services with the aid of an Internet connection, laptop or cellphone, microphone, and webcam (mostly embedded). With video conferencing, you are able to share a screen with other participants, which keeps you virtually connected.

Video conferencing has ruled the corporate world for a decade, and its application is skyrocketing constantly. The impact of this technology has become so widespread that 36% of US white-collar professionals prefer a video conferencing capability in the workplace, or at home, over a pay raise.

This technology has been beneficial for both companies and employees. Along from providing flexibility and saving time on both ends, video conferencing offers several other benefits.

- **Enhanced Communication:** Video conferencing has enhanced communication among businesses and their employees, who are in different locations or time zones.

Important events, schedules, and meetings can be seamlessly conducted with a large team over a video call. The integrated chat option with the service also enhances communication.

- **Manage Expenses and Time**: Business travel can cost a lot of time, money, and resources, both for the company and the employee. A simple switch to a video conference is potent in negotiating deals and saving money on fuel, expensive lunches, or traveling to another city for short meetings.

- **Enhanced Productivity:** With video calls, most of the participants are compelled to stay focused and get straight to the point. Participants are in sync with each other and it promotes brevity and straightforwardness. This is extremely pragmatic for completing projects faster. Also, with video conference meetings, we are assuming that you are working from home. This gives you more time, attention, and a comfortable environment to work in more efficiently.

Freelancers and Digital Nomads

Freelancing is no longer a destitution when it comes to earning a steady income and having a stable job. In fact, it is the new euphemism for a progressive and exciting career that offers new opportunities with each passing day. Not only can you work from the comfort of your own home, but you also have the freedom of choosing your own schedule and taking days off as you please. A major part of this flexibility and prerogative can be attributed to the rise of technology and invention of conducive digital tools.

Freelancers and digital nomads (someone who works remotely to access the benefits of flexibility and time management) have risen in number over the past five years due to the advancement in technology and digital tools, such as video conferencing services, project management software, and other necessary tools specific to particular domains (cloud communications and productivity tools). This has also led multiple companies to embrace the concept of hiring more and more freelancers and digital nomads. In the beginning, people were in constant fear of running out of money or ending up nowhere, which led to only the 'adventurous' professionals to seek freelancing. But since numerous companies are supporting this apprehension, experts of all fields are quitting their full-time office jobs and becoming digital nomads to work from the comfort of their homes.

Since the advent of video conferencing, most freelancers, and even businessmen, have been utilizing this pragmatic tool that offers numerous benefits. Firstly, these services bolster the thought of most professionals - "A meeting that could have been an email."

Video conferencing not only helps to reduce your commute time but also saves part of your paycheck. Since these services are taking a new dimension, freelancers and digital nomads are able to communicate effectively with their clients all around the world. In fact, freelancers should use this prevailing tool more often to conduct virtual meetings with their clients on a regular basis. This not only portrays your seriousness regarding your work but also provides an assurance or proof of getting work done, along with proof of who you are.

Here are a few other prominent reasons why you should make use of this favorable service more often as a freelancer:

- **Elevate your Brand Identity:** With regular video conference calls, you get an opportunity to formally greet your clients every now and then. Connecting with your clients virtually can build a trusting bond through a subtle display of expression and knowing each other face-to-face. This approach is more than just a face for your brand. It adds personality and substance to your brand image.
- **Learn More:** Emails and forwarded documents are usually concise and to the point. While these are typically useful in keeping deadlines and details straightforward, you can also learn a thing or two about a project on a video call. This provides additional details that can revamp the assignment entirely.
- **Share Results:** Quite often, the results or reports you share through emails are indecipherable. The person receiving them might consider them redundant due to difficulties in understanding. This is when video conferencing can be used to advantage. You can personalize your video calls and explain complicated data to your clients through features like screen sharing and real-time chat operations. As soon as your clients are offered a better understanding and are made aware of the highlights of the results or reports, they can see the work for what it is and continue their future agreements with you.

Video conferencing is an absolute boon for freelancers and digital nomads. These virtual wage earners can effortlessly hold virtual meetings and schedule face-to-face appointments. It is specifically favorable for those who reside on the other side of the globe. Let's not forget the huge amount of money that can be saved by avoiding insignificant cross-city and cross-country trips.

Social Distance: The New Challenge

Currently, the world is facing a mortifying pandemic and most people are advised to stay at home to prevent COVID-19 from spreading further. This horrific situation has not only ruined normal business operations but has also impacted our social lives. Large-scale conferences and events, such as Milan Design Week, Google's annual developer's conference, tech and music festival SXSW, major sports events like Formula 1, and even the Olympics have been canceled this year to avoid public gatherings and respect the norms of social distancing.

In this situation, people are trying to conduct business, conferences, and necessary meetings through video calls. A few months ago, video conferencing services were mere conveniences or added benefits to any work environment but with the obligation of social distancing, these have quickly become a necessity. Employees have to work from home, and video calls are one of the ways to stay connected with your boss, colleagues, clients or students if you are a teacher. Students are duty-bound to learn online, though lessens that are conducted over video conferences. Because of this, teachers, businessmen, lawyers, and most employees in general, are trying to learn this new technology.

Enter Zoom. This name was barely known across the world before COVID-19 struck and pushed people to stay at home. Almost every business, school, university, and informal party started using Zoom, which led to a massive surge in its popularity, so much so, that the company noted 2.2 million new users every month over the past few months (since the lockdown measures were established). Its overnight success made it a popular name in every household. It's almost a given that you have heard the name a few times during this lockdown.

If you aren't entirely familiar with it, let us break it down for you. Zoom is a video conferencing platform that allows multiple users to access relevant video conference meetings at the same time. Whether it is your office meeting, or a virtual gathering with your long-distance family, Zoom can keep you connected at all times.

In the past, Zoom was only confined to big corporations, businesses with large teams, or companies that worked with virtual assistants or digital nomads. With the recent practice of social distancing, most of the companies and clients are switching to Zoom to stay connected and keep the work flowing. While companies that require a physical presence have suffered tremendously, video conferences have greatly aided the companies that are able to work virtually.

The following chapters will provide a detailed description of Zoom and teach you how to begin using this handy tool today.

Chapter 1: Introduction to Zoom

As you know by now, Zoom is a cloud-based video conference platform that allows multiple users to access virtual meetings and gatherings at the same time. You can access the service through its website URL or by downloading a mobile application.

Zoom was launched in 2011, but has recently garnered a lot of attention due to the coronavirus pandemic frenzy. Whether it is for online classes, business meetings, informal gatherings, or group practices, Zoom seems to be the number-one tool for staying connected to the outside world amidst this gloomy quarantine. And, with the numerous entertaining and unique features, it is highly preferred when compared to the other video conferencing services.

Since its launch, Zoom has actually been very popular in Europe and the United States but has also boomed all across the world. Unlike other video conferencing services that allow no more than 4 to 5 people to share a screen at one time, Zoom allows hundreds of participants at a time (based on your subscription plan).

But, with so many other video conferencing services available, what is the appeal of Zoom, and what has led people to using this platform more than other services? Apart from its riveting features, it all boils down to its reliability and accessibility.

Chapter 2: Basic Features of Zoom

Group Conferences

Zoom's main objective or concept is its large-scale video conferences and one-on-one meetings. With the free version of Zoom, you can add up to 100 participants and conduct a video conference that lasts up to 40 minutes. If you purchase the 'large meeting' plan, you can add up to 500 participants.

Individual Meetings

Just like any other video conferencing service, Zoom allows you to host one-on-one meetings or individual video calls.

Screen Sharing

The screen sharing feature has become a necessity and provides a lot of convenience. Conducting meetings is simpler when you can show others what you are seeing. You can also have a one-on-one meet-and-greet with preferred individuals through the feature of screen sharing.

Other basic features include:

- Start or end a video call
- Join a meeting
- Mute or unmute the mic
- Invite others

- In-meeting chat
- Record a meeting
- Change your screen name

If you are using the desktop app version, you can also access these features:

- Create polls
- Share your video conference on Facebook Live
- Start a Recording

Chapter 3: General Overview

This chapter will cover the general overview concerning all aspects of Zoom - the setups, subscription plans, plugins and extensions, extra features, and ways to use the app. It will also address the recent data breach and security accusations made about Zoom, to give you more information, and put your mind at ease. Read on to understand how to use this service with utmost privacy.

Setups

Now, there are two types of setup available on this platform: Zoom Meeting and Zoom Room. The former is focused on meetings that are held on this platform, and the latter is a hardware setup that is used for scheduling these Zoom Meetings. You need an additional subscription to access Zoom Room.

Let's take a look at both of these setups individually for more understanding.

Zoom Meeting

As the name suggests, Zoom Meeting is a setup that hosts multiple users at the same time and allows seamless video conferencing to conduct important meetings or to host informal virtual gatherings. Even if you don't have a Zoom account, you can access this platform to join a Zoom Meeting. These meetings are attainable through devices such as laptops and phones, and a webcam or a video conferencing camera.

Zoom Room

As explained, Zoom Room is accessible from conference rooms and can assist in scheduling Zoom Meetings and virtual discussions. Basically, this hardware system used to operate Zoom Meetings is driven by dedicated software that is extremely simple to use. With a touch of a button, you can schedule, launch, and run a Zoom Meeting. This setup is beneficial for companies with large teams that need frequent discussions.

This service offers you a 30-day trial before purchasing the full subscription of Zoom Room. It lets you determine its efficiency and utility before you make a purchase decision. To buy this plan, you will be paying $49 per month.

For a Zoom Room setup, you need the following tools:

- A computer or laptop to sync, launch, and run Zoom Meetings
- A microphone, a speaker, and video conference camera
- 1 or 2 HDTV monitors to screen-share important presentations and display participants
- An HDMI cable to connect the TV monitors and computer screens
- An internet cable and a stable internet connection, or reliable Wi-Fi
- A tablet for participants to launch and run the Zoom Meetings

Subscription Plans

The platform offers 4 types of subscription plans based on the number of participants, duration of the meeting, and the amount of cloud storage that is offered.

1. **Zoom Free (Level 1):** As the name suggests, you can access this plan for free. This level has the ability to host up to 100 participants at a time and conduct a meeting that can last up to 40 minutes. However, you cannot record the meetings.

2. **Zoom Pro (Level 2):** This level lets you create personal meeting IDs, record the meetings in your device's cloud, and conduct meetings up to 24 hours. You, as a host, will be charged $14.99 per month.

3. **Zoom Business (Level 3):** Apart from the basic features, Zoom Business lets you host meetings using your company's branding and specific URLs. Also, you can access the transcripts of the recordings in the cloud. What's more? You are eligible for customer support. You, as a host, will be charged $19.99 per month for Zoom Business.

4. **Zoom Enterprise (Level 4):** This plan is ideal for companies that have more than 1,000 employees. You get unlimited cloud storage and special discounts on webinars. You are also eligible for a discount on Zoom Room. A customer success manager is dedicated to your service. You, as a host, will be charged $19.99 per month for Zoom Business.

The fifth level is Zoom Room, which we already discussed above.

This image will provide a better understanding of the definite segregation of each tier.

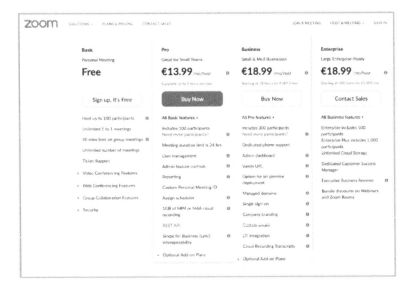

Zoom App

Zoom can also be accessed through its desktop and mobile application version. The desktop app version can be downloaded on Windows and macOS, and the mobile application can be downloaded on iOS and Android.

While it is possible to access any Zoom meeting without signing up and creating an account, it is advisable to sign up using a Google, Facebook, or Zoom account if you will use it frequently. This will make it easier to access every time you want to conduct a meeting.

Get Started with Zoom

Before we learn about accessing and starting Zoom Meetings, the best way to learn about it is through downloading and installing the Zoom app. This will simplify its accessibility factor. Whether you are hosting a meeting or attending as a participant, using Zoom can be extremely effortless once you follow these steps.

As a Host

Download the App:

Download the Zoom App (desktop or mobile app version), you can type in the browser *https://zoom.us/download* to go to the download page. Follow the steps and once downloaded on your computer, create an account, or login with your Facebook or Google account.

If you are using your computer or laptop, you will see this window below as soon as you enter.

Upon using a mobile app, an interface like this will pop up as soon as you enter.

For easier understanding, we are assuming that you are using the desktop version of Zoom.

START A NEW MEETING

If you are hosting a meeting, click on the 'New Meeting' option that is represented by the orange icon. You will enter an interface that enables you to change the settings according to your preferences.

AUDIO SETTINGS

First, you will tweak the audio settings. To begin with, find the 'Join Audio' at the bottom-left corner of the window and click the arrow beside it. Click on 'Audio Settings' from the dropdown menu.

A 'Settings' window will pop up, which will look like this.

You can always access to this window by clicking on the setting icon on the top right part of the screen

- Once the window pops up, click on the dropdown list located on the right side of 'Test Speaker' and select the speaker you prefer. You can either choose your headphone jack, your device's speaker, or any other speaker that is linked externally. We would recommend that you wear headphones as it will block out background noise, and keep your meeting private if other people are around.

- Next, you should check the microphone quality. Click on the dropdown menu on the right side of 'Test Mic.' Depending on the microphone device you are using, select the relevant option. If you have an external microphone connected to your system, the list will display the name. If not, select 'same as system' to use the device's microphone.

- Then, you will check the input level of your microphone and voice quality. Start talking and view the slider besides 'Input Level' as it transitions from red to green. Your audio is stable if you are in the green zone (not too slow and not too loud). Check the box besides 'Automatically adjust microphone volume' to make it easier.

- Leave the other settings as they are. You can probably check the box that says 'Join audio by computer when joining a meeting' to access the same setup as soon as you join a call.

VIDEO SETTINGS

Now, we will tweak the video settings. Click on 'Video' located above 'Audio' in the left panel.

The Video Settings box will look like this.

- As soon as you click on 'Video', a box appears with a message saying, 'Zoom would like to access the camera.' Click on 'OK.' The black box in this picture will display what is seen by your front-facing camera. This is how the other participants will see you during the call. You can adjust your position and device to provide a clear view.
- If you have other devices or webcams attached externally to your video interface, select the device from the dropdown menu besides 'Camera.' Leave the other settings as they are, and exit the box.

STOP VIDEO OPTION

Once your audio and video settings are in place, you are good to go. Close the setting page and click on the button "New Meeting" to start a meeting. If you need the call to be just audio, you can select the 'Stop Video' option on the bottom-left corner of the window, as you access to the meeting.

INVITE NEW PARTICIPANTS

The next step will involve inviting participants to the call. Select the 'Participants' option on the bottom panel of the window, and then click on "Invite".

You will see a window that looks like this.

You can either invite people from your contact list or via email. The easiest way is to click on 'Copy URL' and send the generated meeting URL with the people you wish to invite. Exit the box. Once you send this URL to the preferred participants, they can easily access the meeting by pasting this URL in their browser. You can also text or send the meeting password to your participants to join the discussion. We will elaborate further on this later in this section.

MANAGE PARTICIPANTS

We will now manage the participants that have permission to access the meeting. Click on 'Participants' on the bottom panel of the main window.

You will see a popup that will display all the participants that have entered the meeting. It will look like this.

- If you move your mouse over the participants' names, you can mute a particular participant or mute all of them by selecting 'Mute All' at the bottom. This functionality is extremely useful when a single person is in needs to speak or is instructing everyone.

Chat options

Access the 'Chat' option on the bottom of the main window. It will open popup window. This will allow you to write comments and send messages during the meeting. You can also upload files or photos from your device, Google Drive, or Dropbox by clicking on the file icon.

This is particularly convenient if you want to discuss certain specifications during the meeting, such as presentations, reports, or diagrams. In case you wish to send a private message to a participant you will need to click on "everyone" and select from the list the person that you wish to contact.

Record a meeting

To record the meeting, select 'Record' at the bottom of the main window. As soon as you click the option, you will notice a red pulsing icon in the top-left corner of the window. This signal shows that the meeting is being recorded. The participants will also be aware of the recording as the red icon will be displayed beside your name in the vertical window on the right side of the screen. You can also stop or pause the recording by clicking on the respective buttons beside the recording icon.

To access the recording and choose a particular location to save the recorded data, select 'zoom.us' on the top panel of your window and go to 'Preferences'.

Next, select 'Recording' in the left panel. Click on the list beside 'Store my recordings at,' select 'Choose a new location,' and select the folder or location that will collect all the recordings.

SHARE YOUR SCREEN

To share your screen with other participants, click on the green icon depicting 'Share Screen' at the bottom of the main window.

A window like this will appear.

When this window pops up, you can choose the desktop or screen that you want to share with others. As soon as you click on 'Share', a window saying 'Allow Zoom to share your screen' will pop up. Click on 'Open System Preferences' and select 'Zoom' from the list.

END THE MEETING

To end the meeting or the exit, select 'End Meeting,' denoted in red in the bottom-right corner. Select 'End Meeting for All' from the pop-up window to end the meeting.

SCHEDULE A MEETING

Now let's try scheduling the next meeting, go to the main page of your app and click on the icon that says 'Schedule.'

You will see a window like this.

- Type the name of the subject, class, or topic of discussion of the meeting in the 'Topic' box. Select the starting and ending date and time of the meeting. Since we are learning the features on the free version of Zoom, you can set a duration of only 40 minutes. To increase the duration, go to the official website and buy a subscription plan that offers longer meetings and additional benefits.

- Next, select the box beside 'Generate Automatically' under 'Meeting ID' (this should be your preferred option).

- Then, generate a password by checking the box besides 'Require meeting password.' Type a password of your choosing and share it with the other participants to give them access to the meeting. By unchecking the box, anyone can access the meeting without a password, so, it's always preferable to create a password.

- Next, you can select whether you want your video to be on or off during the meeting. You also have the option to choose whether you want your participants' video to be on or off.

- For the audio, select 'Telephone and Computer Audio,' as some of your participants might use their phone and cellular data if they don't have a stable broadband connection.

- You can add this schedule reminder on a calendar of your choice. Choose among iCal, Google Calendar, or any other calendar that you use.

- Lastly, click on Advanced Options and select your preferred option among 'Enable waiting room' (lets your participants wait before starting the meeting), 'Enable join before host' (lets your participants enter the meeting before you do), 'Mute participants on entry' (mutes all participants until you enter and unmute), and 'Record the meeting automatically on the local computer' (begins recording without selecting the option).

Once you select the appropriate options, click on 'Schedule' and your meeting will be noted on your calendar. When you open your calendar, you will receive the details regarding the meeting, including the meeting ID, password, and even a mobile tap feature that takes you to the meeting directly if accessed through a cell phone. Send this auto-generated message containing the meeting details to your desired participants through e-mail or text.

Home page Options

A few more options that can be accessed from the home page (located on the top of the page) include:

- **Chat:** If you have made a few friends on Zoom and added them, they will appear on this Chat on a panel. You can directly chat with them through this option.
- **Meetings:** With this option, you can check all the meetings that you have scheduled for a future date or the ones that have been scheduled for you by someone else. The panel will also show your Personal Meeting ID or PMI. With your PMI, you can use options such as Copy Invitation, Edit, or Join from a Room.
- **Contacts:** You can view your added contacts in this panel, both from your directory and channels.
- **Your profile:** You can change your profile settings by selecting your picture icon on the top-right corner of the home page. This is basically your avatar. You can add a personal note, set your status as Away, Available, or Do Not Disturb (you can choose the duration), make changes to your profile, and upgrade to the Pro version.

As a Participant

Follow "**Start a new meeting**" as mentioned above.

Step 2: Tweak the audio, video, and recording settings as explained above.

Step 3: To join a particular meeting, you can either copy and paste the given URL into your browser, or enter the meeting password after logging in. The password is a 9-digit number that is generated when a host creates a meeting.

- If you have the meeting URL, go to your web browser, paste the URL, and press Enter. If you have already downloaded the Zoom app, you will be asked if you want to be directed to Zoom. If not, it will open the window in your browser.

Once you press Enter, you will see something like this.

- If you have the meeting password, log in to Zoom or open the Zoom app and click on 'Join.' Type in your meeting password and your name. Click on Join.

Step 4: Use 'Mute/Unmute' or 'Start/Stop Video' at the bottom of the screen as you wish. If you swipe left, you will have an option that says 'Tap to Speak' in the center of the screen. Tap on the circle when you want to speak and release to mute it automatically.

Step 5: To chat, update Meeting Settings, change the background, or to raise your hand to speak, tap on 'More' in the bottom-right corner. Select the option you want to change.

Step 6: To exit a meeting, tap on 'End Meeting' on the bottom-right corner. Select 'Leave Meeting' in the window that appears, which will allow you to exit. The meeting will continue until everyone leaves individually or until the host presses 'End Meeting for All.' If you are using a mobile device, tap on 'Leave' denoted in the red in the top-right corner of the screen.

Chapter 4: Advanced Tips

Now that you are aware about the general overview and basic features of this platform, let's dig deeper. This chapter will embrace the advanced features and additional tips that can be accessed within this service.

Change your Background Theme

This feature is a fun way to add some drama and humor to your conference calls. You can choose from multiple background themes such as a beach, an ocean view, cityscapes, outer space, and even popular meme templates. All you have to do is go to Settings, select Virtual Background, and choose the background theme you prefer. You can also upload an image of your choice. This is a great option if you have failed to clean or organize your house and don't want to display your messy room to others.

To use this option on a mobile application, join a meeting, tap on the three dots at the bottom of the screen, and choose 'More.' You will find a 'Virtual Background' option. Tap on it to change your backdrop or upload an image of your choice.

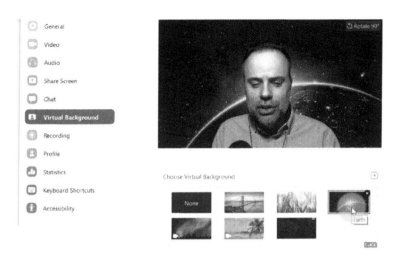

You can also create your own background to represent your brand by displaying your company's logo or mission statement. The main benefit of a virtual backdrop is that you don't have to worry about your messy surroundings while attending a video call.

Use Keyboard Shortcuts

Keyboard shortcuts are extremely handy if you dislike hovering over the screen with a mouse. Basic functions, such as sharing your screen, recording your screen, switching to a full screen preview, and joining a meeting can be achieved with keyboard shortcuts.

Here are the basic keyboard shortcuts for regular operations (based on a MacBook keyboard layout):

Meeting Shortcuts

- **Command (⌘) +J**: Join Meeting
- **Command (⌘) +Control+V**: Start Meeting

- **Command (⌘) +J**: Schedule Meeting
- **Command (⌘) +Control+S**: Screen Share via Direct Share
- **Command (⌘) +Shift+A**: Mute/unmute audio
- **Command (⌘) +Control+M**: Mute audio for everyone except the host (only available to the host)
- **Command (⌘) +Control+U**: Unmute audio for everyone except host (only available to the host)
- **Space:** Push to talk
- **Command (⌘) +Shift+V**: Start/stop video
- **Command (⌘) +Shift+N**: Switch camera
- **Command (⌘) +Shift+S**: Start/stop screen share
- **Command (⌘) +Shift+T:** Pause or resume screen share
- **Command (⌘) +Shift+R**: Start local recording
- **Command (⌘) +Shift+C**: Start cloud recording
- **Command (⌘) +Shift+P:** Pause or resume recording

Chat Shortcuts

- **Command (⌘) +K**: Jump to chat with someone
- **Command (⌘) +T**: Screenshot

General Shortcuts

- **Command (⌘) +W:** Close the current window
- **Command (⌘) +L:** Switch to Portrait or Landscape View, depending on current view
- **Ctrl+T**: Switch from one tab to the next

However, there are certain prerequisites to use these keyboard shortcuts, which are:

- Windows Desktop Client Version **3.5.19869.0701** or higher
- Mac Desktop Client Version **3.5.19877.0701** or higher
- Linux Desktop Client Version **1.1.32904.1120** or higher
- iPad with iOS App Version **4.4.5 (55341.0715)** or higher

You can also edit the keyboard shortcuts based on your preference by going to Settings and then Accessibility. Click on the shortcut and press the shortcut key to edit it.

Emoji Reactions

Emojis in Zoom conferences are mostly used for enhanced and fun communication. In informal meetings, emojis are considered to be a fun element that can be accessed for communication without disturbing or interrupting the meeting. This is specifically useful when you are knowingly or unintentionally muted during the call.

To access emojis, tap on the Reactions tab located at the bottom of the screen and tap on the emoji you want to react with. If you want to customize your emojis, access the Zoom desktop app. These also show your presence and focus within a discussion when your call organizer or host accesses the nonverbal feedback feature. Your emoji will appear beside your name, which is visible by all participants in the call. Simple emojis like a 'thumbs up' or a 'happy face' are easy to use for communication.

'Touch Up My Appearance'

This additional beauty filter is useful when you are just out of bed and need to attend an important meeting. It provides a dewy and filtered touch-up to your face, offering a fresh look. At times, video calls can alter your look despite dressing up and wearing makeup. This is when the beauty feature can come in handy. It makes you look well-rested by smoothing your facial features.

To access this feature, tap the up arrow that is located next to the Start Video button and click on Video Settings. You will find 'Touch Up My Appearance' below My Video. Check the box and you are good to go.

Annotations

This feature can be accessed on the floating panel while sharing your screen. Annotations are often overlooked by most of the users but can be extremely useful. Click on 'Annotations,' located on the left side of 'More.' Another panel with all annotating features will appear below the main floating panel.

Here are some important features on this panel that you could use during the meeting:

- Spotlight: Upon clicking Spotlight, a red dot will appear that can be toggled with your mouse. With this spotlight, you can point out important parts of the shared screen, making it easier for your participants to follow.
- Arrow: Consider this feature to be the 'sticky note' of Zoom calls. You can place an arrow on any important points in the shared screen. The arrow will display the

user's name, making other participants aware of who emphasized which point.

- Undo, Redo, and Clear: It is as clear as it seems. You can undo, redo, and delete all annotations that you made on the screen.

- Stamp: This is another form of Arrow that lets you add permanent arrows on important points without displaying your name.

- Along with these options, you can also add text or draw on the screen.

Record Transcripts

The audio of your meetings can be transcribed and saved to the cloud. If you are a host, you can access the highlights of the meeting by using these transcripts. You can scan and edit these to filter important data from the meetings. To use this feature, go to My Meeting Settings after signing in to the web portal of this platform. Next, go to Recording and choose the Cloud Recording option. Then, enable the Audio Transcript feature. Verify it before you go back.

PREVENT ZOOM BOMBINGS

Zoom bombings are the result of the penetration of any uninvited user within the meeting in the intention of interrupting the meeting or ruining it. At times, users can enter a meeting accidentally. If the meeting is important or concerns professional business, it is necessary to prevent Zoom bombing.

Follow these steps to prevent Zoom bombing as a host.

1. Create a Zoom meeting and prepare a password by tapping on 'Require Meeting Password' under the Password section. Create a strong password and share it with the participants who are scheduled for the meeting. Any user without a password will be unable to join the meeting.

2. If you are using the Waiting Room feature, you can let the participants in one by one. To enable this feature, tap on Advanced Settings after signing in and check the 'Enable Waiting Room' box.

3. If you do not want any of your participants to share the screen, tap on Advanced Sharing Options after clicking on the arrow beside 'Share Screen.' You will be shown these questions, "How many participants can share at the same time?" And "Who can share?" For the former, select "One participant can share at a time" and for the other question, select "Only host."

4. Finally, go to Manage Participants in the Zoom toolbar (which shows all the active participants in the meeting) and click on 'More' (located at the bottom right hand part). Click on 'Lock Meeting.' By selecting this option, all users out of this room will be barred from entering, even if they are provided with the password of the meeting.

HIDE FLOATING PANEL WHILE SHARING YOUR SCREEN

When sharing your screen that shows your web browser, the floating panel might make it difficult to toggle between the tabs. It is possible to accidentally click on 'Stop Sharing' from the floating panel as it covers the tabs on your screen. To avoid this situation, go to 'More' on the floating panel once you have started sharing your screen and click on 'Hide Floating Meeting Controls' to hide the panel.

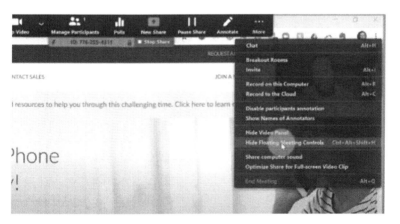

With this option, you can easily navigate between tabs as the floating panel is no longer interrupting the browser interface. To get the floating menu back on your screen, press Esc.

Zoom Data Breach and Security Accusations

The recent accusations of data breach and infiltration in Zoom has led many people to switch to other services. There were reports of bugs in the URL generation that let hackers eavesdrop on private conversations, security issues in the Windows 10 build, and phone data being sent to Facebook even with the absence of a social media account. Upon the revelation of these accusations, Zoom ensured that they were implementing an end-to-end encryption that provided critical security. However, it was found that a substandard AES-128 key in ECB mode was used. This has caused speculations among users and top companies like Google, the New York City Department of Education, and Australian and German governments have stopped its use. These bodies will revert to this service after complete assurance of security and privacy is provided by the currently-popular video conferencing service.

How has Zoom Coped with these Data Breach Accusations?

As expected, Zoom tried to clean up its mess, as much as it could. To make up for these mistakes, the platform will no longer serve meeting ID numbers in the address bars. Moreover, an additional security tab can be accessed by hosts and participants to provide adequate security settings. Also, the service has stepped up to provide secure geofencing measures to provide the option of entering and exiting out of particular data center regions. These norms were recently established, and the service is taking further measures to make the platform more secure and private for use.

While using this service, you can take a few measures to ensure further security while attending a call.

- **Create a Password:** This is the simplest way to make sure that no unknown user infiltrates your meeting and space. It takes no time at all to create a password and forward it to your participants. Do this to prevent your call from being hacked. Whether it's a group call, one-on-one meeting, or your account settings, you can create a password and protect your virtual space. We already learned how to create and send a password to your team members. If you are a paid user, you can go to 'Group Management' and direct every participant to follow the same password-protection guidelines.

- **Do Not Allow Participants to Share their Screen:** Unless it's extremely necessary, turn off the option that allows your invitees to share their screen. This will reduce the chances of your video call being infiltrated by hackers and avoid embarrassing screen shares, particularly during formal meetings or while hosting a class. Go to the 'Security' tab while the meeting is active and select the relevant option.

- **Enable the Waiting Room Feature:** While this isn't entirely related to privacy, it does bring a sense of controlled security for the overall session to the host.

- **Remove Users That Cause Nuisance:** As we learned, you can remove a particular user by accessing the 'More' option and removing them from the meeting. In case you don't want them to join, you can disable the option 'Allow Removed Participants to Rejoin by going to 'Settings,'

'Meetings,' and then 'Basic.' This is particularly helpful if you are conducting an online class with several students.

- **Do Not Generate your Own ID:** Let Zoom generate an ID for you. There is a higher chance of any known or unknown user deciphering your ID through several means (it can be shared publicly by mistake, or you could be hacked). Every time you schedule a meeting, let Zoom generate the ID for you.

- **Lock your Meeting:** Once all your participants are present in the room, lock the meeting to avoid infiltration. To do this, go to 'Manage Participants,' tap on 'More,' and select 'Lock.' Make sure that you follow this procedure after all your expected participants have arrived in the room.

- **Check for Updates Regularly:** This is probably the most important tip of all. As we know, Zoom is working to provide safer access to its service with enhanced security features and tools that ensure minimal chances of data leaks. Zoom will likely add bug-fixes or deploy certain security measures with each update. Keep on checking for updates now and again. To do this, open the desktop app, click on your profile that is located on the top-right corner of the home page, and tap on 'Check for Updates.'

All in all, you can depend on Zoom to conduct video conferences. The company has promised better and updated security clauses in the future, and you can rely on it for future use as well. Plus, Zoom's support team has been incredulously impressive. It is globally known for its user support due to the availability of customer care voice controls in almost every time zone.

CHAPTER 5: HOW TO BE A PRO IN VIDEO CONFERENCES

Until a cure for COVID-19 is found, people around the world need to be careful and stay at home to prevent further spread. The time required to flatten this pandemic's curve is still uncertain. This means that we might be quarantined for a while.

Now that you learned everything about Zoom, you can begin exploring its benefits. However, if you are planning on using it frequently and specifically for formal purposes, you should be a pro at it. While learning all practical aspects are necessary to run video conferences like a boss, you should also reflect on certain contextual aspects that will make you an expert on all spectrums.

A bad webcam, dull lighting, poor connectivity, and the inability to operate a video call is surely off-putting. But, worse that that is a lack of authority and leadership when hosting a meeting. As a leader, you don't want that, do you?

Here are a few tips to help you become a pro in video conferences:

Commit to Virtual Working

Virtual working, or working from home, isn't always as easy as it sounds. Sure, you have the flexibility and more time to get things done, but this might actually lead you into a spiral of procrastination.

For this to work, you need to commit. Now, this can be a challenge if you are new to it or are handling a large team. Handling and committing to a virtual working environment can be boiled down to two things: effective communication skills and enhanced productivity.

Let's dig deeper.

- As a boss, handling a team, particularly a virtually-working team, can be one of the biggest challenges in the corporate world. The first thing you can do is encourage communication within the team. Make sure that your employees or colleagues are aware of the difference between a virtual working environment and an office job. Explain basic details, such as how you will communicate and what that looks like. An example can be holding trial video conferences to ensure effective communication in the future.
- Keep the video conferences concise. You can automatically enhance productivity by sticking to the point and explaining the project objectives in a precise manner. This will provide a clear explanation of your ideas and your employees or colleagues will not be caught up in frequent video conferences.

Importance of Scheduling

Scheduling is important even if you are working remotely. In fact, it might be more important if you tend to procrastinate or have a habit of delaying submissions and assignments. With proper scheduling, you can respect deadlines and get work on time. Treat your home as your workplace. When it comes to video conferences, schedule your calls beforehand and inform the required participants about the meeting details. This should include the meeting ID or password (to enter the meeting), the topic of discussion, time, date, and duration of the meeting. Having prior knowledge of the meeting will ensure that your participants are thoroughly prepared and ready to actively engage in the conference.

Even though it might seem unimportant, scheduling does help keep track of your operations, especially if you need to consult your team occasionally. Set reminders to alert you an hour before your meeting. You don't want to be late to a meeting that you host.

Set Goals

Working from home, without physical assistance from your team, is tough. When you want to continue your business, you need to constantly consult and gel with your team. This is not entirely possible while working virtually. To be as effective as possible, you should set certain goals. Whether it relates to your year-end turnover or establishing communication within your team, a set of objectives will help you when you are working at a distance. Set goals, host a meeting, and communicate to your team over a video conference. You may need to spend hours in the planning stages before you begin communicating with your employees.

Trim these goals into processes and tasks and assign them to relevant employees and departments. Try to simplify the tasks as much as possible to maintain coordination among your team members. Keep a track of the tasks that you have assigned to your team members and stay connected virtually at all times. Ensure clarity between your team members and conduct 'after-action' reviews once the deadlines are reached.

This practice might take up to 90 days for it to become routine, but once you do, you will close in on your target. Conduct trial sessions in between to keep the workflow stable. Since there is a lack of constant communication and observation, ensuring productivity can be difficult. Hold regular review meetings and convey your expectations about intermediate milestones despite a lack of face-to-face communication.

The point is, you may need to learn to micro-manage to be a true leader with virtual meetings.

Do's and Don'ts

Assuming that you are on a formal call, there are certain dos and don'ts you should follow as an active participant.

Dos

- **Create an Appropriate Setup:** No one wants to look at a messy background when they are talking to you on a video call. Needless to say, a clean backdrop is mandatory to conduct any video call. After you clean your surroundings, start the video camera to test how your video call looks and to ensure that your backdrop is appropriate. Set the camera at an appropriate angle. Keep it at eye level to ensure that the other person can see you with ease. Ask family members or roommates to keep quiet until the video conference ends, or remove yourself

44

from a noisy environment. Next, check the lighting. A backlight can be extremely uncomfortable and distracting for the other person. Stick to natural lighting or overhead lighting.

- **Pay Attention and Stay Focused:** Staying focused is necessary while on a video call because failing to do so can show a sincere lack of professionalism. Try not to send emails, look elsewhere, and don't check your phone. Many people have a habit of constantly looking at themselves on the screen. This shows a lack of attention to the other person and you could come across as self-centered. Even if you have to look away, communicate it to the person who is on the call with you and excuse yourself for a second. However, try not to do that in the first place. Since you are more visible on video conferences when compared to physical meetings, people will notice when you are distracted.

- **Mute the Call when the Other Person is speaking:** By muting a call, the other person can talk freely without being disturbed. This is particularly useful during group conference calls. Participants can become easily distracted due to unwanted noises in the background, which is why you should mute yourself when you are not speaking. Consider switching off your video too. If someone interrupts your call or if you need to tend to something, switching off your video is convenient. However, at times, the other person is unable to focus with switched-off video screens. Ask their permission first and act accordingly.

- **Be Courteous:** Needless to say, you should be courteous to the other callers and display basic manners while the call is ongoing. Introduce yourself and ask others for their names as well. Try to remember as many as you can and address them by their name whenever you can.

- **Understand the Difference Between a Video Call and an Email:** Some people fail to understand the importance of a topic of discussion. At times, even if the topic could be successfully discussed over an e-mail or Slack, they decide to host a video conference, which is, in fact, completely unnecessary. Know the difference and stick to an email and you will not waste anyone's time. However, if the subject is intense and needs verbal explanation for full comprehension, do not hesitate to schedule a video conference.

- **Check your Internet Connection and Speed Beforehand:** Before starting or participating in a video call, make sure that your internet setup is adequate. Check the broadband connection and speed. Do a test video call with one of your close acquaintances to ensure the connection.

Don'ts

- **Do Not Interrupt the Other Person:** Constant interruption is off-putting. Wait for your turn. You will know when it is your turn to speak. If there is something urgent or important that needs to be spoken, give a signal and then speak. If your colleagues are planning to host these meetings constantly, work out a set of gestures for permission to speak or ask questions, like raising your hand. You can also use the chat options available in most of the video conferencing services to ask a question or insert a comment without interrupting the flow of the speaker.

- **Do Not Multi-task:** As mentioned, do not cause any distraction during the video call. Multitasking is the worst form of distraction. Basically, eating, checking your phone, talking to someone else, etc., are major forms of distraction that should be avoided at all costs. Wait for the call to end or excuse yourself if it's extremely important.

- **Do Not Look Messy or Sloppy:** Along with a clean backdrop, a clean appearance is also necessary during a video call, particularly during professional meetings. Dressing in your comfiest pajamas and sweatshirt is fine if you are attending a virtual family gathering, but with a professional call, you need to change to formal clothes, at least from the waist up if you are sitting through the entire call. Don't forget to neaten your hair. Dressing for your audience will leave an impression.

An Additional Tip: While conducting or participating in a video conference, agree on one language and stick to it. This is specifically necessary if your video call involves people from all around the globe or for bilingual participants.

CHAPTER 6: THE FUTURE OF VIDEO CONFERENCING

The future of video conferences is bright. In fact, it is bound to become more of a necessity instead of being considered as just an added benefit. The domain of video conferencing has noted a rapid surge in the past 2 to 3 years, with more than 50% of employees and business professionals using one or more services within their workplace. Within the next five to seven years, video conferences will combine the necessity of phone calls and emails, and become a mandatory requirement for most corporations. With groundbreaking technological advances in the modern world, the use of artificial intelligence is improving voice calls and aids voice-command devices in simple tasks. It is believed that video conferencing will improve and grow with a parallel augmentation in artificial intelligence.

The bottom line is, video conferencing is here to stay, and rightly so. As a matter of fact, this niche has just infiltrated the business world; video conferencing in the future will be the new normal, speculated to be assisted by artificial intelligence and robotics for control and voice commands (possibly with more importance than human voice assistants). Currently, technological advancements are also allowing the integration of machine learning within video conferences and online chats. With a similar amelioration, we will be able to analyze data with ease, break cultural and language barriers, and calculate the quantifiable aspects related to one's company.

With the current lockdown situation, most of the employees around the world are forced to work from home. Since most businesses are obligated to conduct virtual meetings during this crisis, the prominence of virtual meeting services is becoming more and more coherent. Video conferencing has proven to be an effective tactic in increasing productivity and saving time and money. This realization is dawning upon most of the business and corporate world.

In fact, a few companies are making Zoom meetings a permanent solution to travel reduction and cost-cutting after realizing the convenience and efficiency it provides. Some of the companies are still skeptical about the productivity and efficiency of working through Zoom meetings, which is why they aren't ready to accept this change yet. However, many companies are looking forward to giving it a try, once things go back to normal.

If this current practice of isolation is normalized, video conferencing will overtake phone calls and emails in the business world, and improve the experience of face-to-face engagement at a distance. And, with the rising affordability of broadband connections and improved webcam quality, this medium is here to stay.

Conclusion

Whether you feel like meeting your friends and collectively having a glass of wine or attending formal meetings and company conferences, Zoom has got you covered. With the devastating pandemic that is affecting millions of people worldwide, it is becoming strenuous for everyone to keep their minds sane. Most of us miss our families and friends and need to connect with them virtually.

If you are planning to open a business as soon as the economy becomes more stable, consider video conferencing services such as Zoom as a crucial part of your working conditions. It can not only save you money but also improve productivity, eventually resulting in decreased turnover and more profits. If you are already running a business, try to incorporate video calls as a part of your regime. And, if you are a current employee of a company, you can suggest this solution to your boss.

When it comes to your family and friends, Zoom is a great way to get everyone together at the same time. You can host a meeting and chat over a glass of wine, organize a game for everyone to play, or create a quiz. The possibilities are endless.

Being a pro at hosting a video conference is important. But what's also important is leading the virtual meeting, especially if you are the host or team leader. However, as a participant, you should also actively participate and make the most out of your presence. Now that you have learned all the features that are available in Zoom, you are trained to use this service with expertise.

To sum it up, Zoom offers excellent support, basic and advanced features that enhance a successful video conference, impressive host and participant controls, thorough engagement, and, now, reliable security, making it a complete package.

With Zoom, you can thoroughly practice social distancing while achieving your daily meeting objectives, all virtually. And, as you have seen, this platform is straightforward and effortless to use. With multiple features and an efficient free plan, you are just a click away from downloading and using this wonderful service that will connect you to the world from the comfort of your home. So, whether it's a Pictionary game with your loved ones or an important business meeting, Zoom will assist you through it.

Have fun video-conferencing!

What Did You Think of Zoom for Beginners?

First of all, thank you for purchasing this book, Zoom for beginners: The absolute step-by-step beginner guide to quickly get started with Zoom and run successful classes and virtual meetings. I know you could have picked any number of books to read, but you picked this book and for that I am extremely grateful.

I hope that it added at value and quality to your everyday life. If so, it would be really nice if you could share this book with your friends and family.

If you enjoyed this book and found some benefit in reading this, I'd like to hear from you and hope that you could take some time to post a review on Amazon. Your feedback and support will help me to greatly improve my writing craft for future projects and make this book even better.

I want you to know that your review is very important and so, if you'd like to **leave a review**, all you have to do is go on Amazon and review your order. I wish you all the best in your future success in your virtual meetings!

Thank you and good luck!

Made in the USA
Coppell, TX
16 September 2020

38023194R00033